THE VISIBLE FIELD

ZOË

RYDER

RIVER RIVER BOOKS *Durham, North Carolina*

WHITE

Praise for THE VISIBLE FIELD

"*The Visible Field* moves with boundless enthusiasm for each moment's last burnishing. These poems let you curl into a space you didn't know existed yet somehow expected. Let's call it the visible field of imagination. Zoë Ryder White knows how to get there. She writes, 'The people in me keep me / up late talking, sometimes / laughing, carrying on.' Every line is a chance to be curious by 'the world, shucked, the world / inside the world.'"

—LAUREN CAMP, author of *An Eye in Each Square*

"Zoë Ryder White's poems are strong and vital and astonishingly satisfying—and they are satisfying not only in their ease of movement from the real world to the symbolic one, their genius for metaphoric transformation, the narrative verve they display, their deep, visually alert representations of nature, their rhetorical keenness and toughness, but also, and most vitally, in their psychological transparency and intimacy. A spectacular book that can be read and read and read again."

—VIJAY SESHADRI, author of *That Was Now, This Is Then*, Winner of the Pulitzer Prize

"*The Visible Field* pays such careful attention to the physical world that it cannot help but expose its concealments. How does this concealment change us? As the poet notes in the opening of 'Interview': 'The fish, when split, had a belly full of plastic, but it was still a fish.' The hollows of the body, the pockets of dresses, vaults, 'I am inside these birds,' Zoë Ryder White writes in one poem; the 'dim rooms' inside a plum that has yet to come to fruition—all these are spaces of containment. In these poems we see that in dealing with attention to the world's physicality, one is always dealing with the possibility of hiddenness.

The body itself might be the greatest and most tactile representation of all that exists between flesh and consciousness, vessel and seed: 'When I was an envelope, I enclosed / a red scrap,' White writes with her subtle grace. In *The Visible Field*, we see that the book *itself* is a casing which hides within itself a field of study: of a life, with its landscapes, children, friends and memories and confinements. Here is hidden *vision,* given to us by a specific poet, whose eye is generous and playful, who coaxes the readers to question the messiness of the whole business of language. 'To read out of order / is to arrange one's affection / deliberately,' one poem posits in its dissolution of the object of a book. I will continue to ponder the idiosyncratic wisdoms of these poems."

—BIANCA STONE, author of *The Near and Distant World*

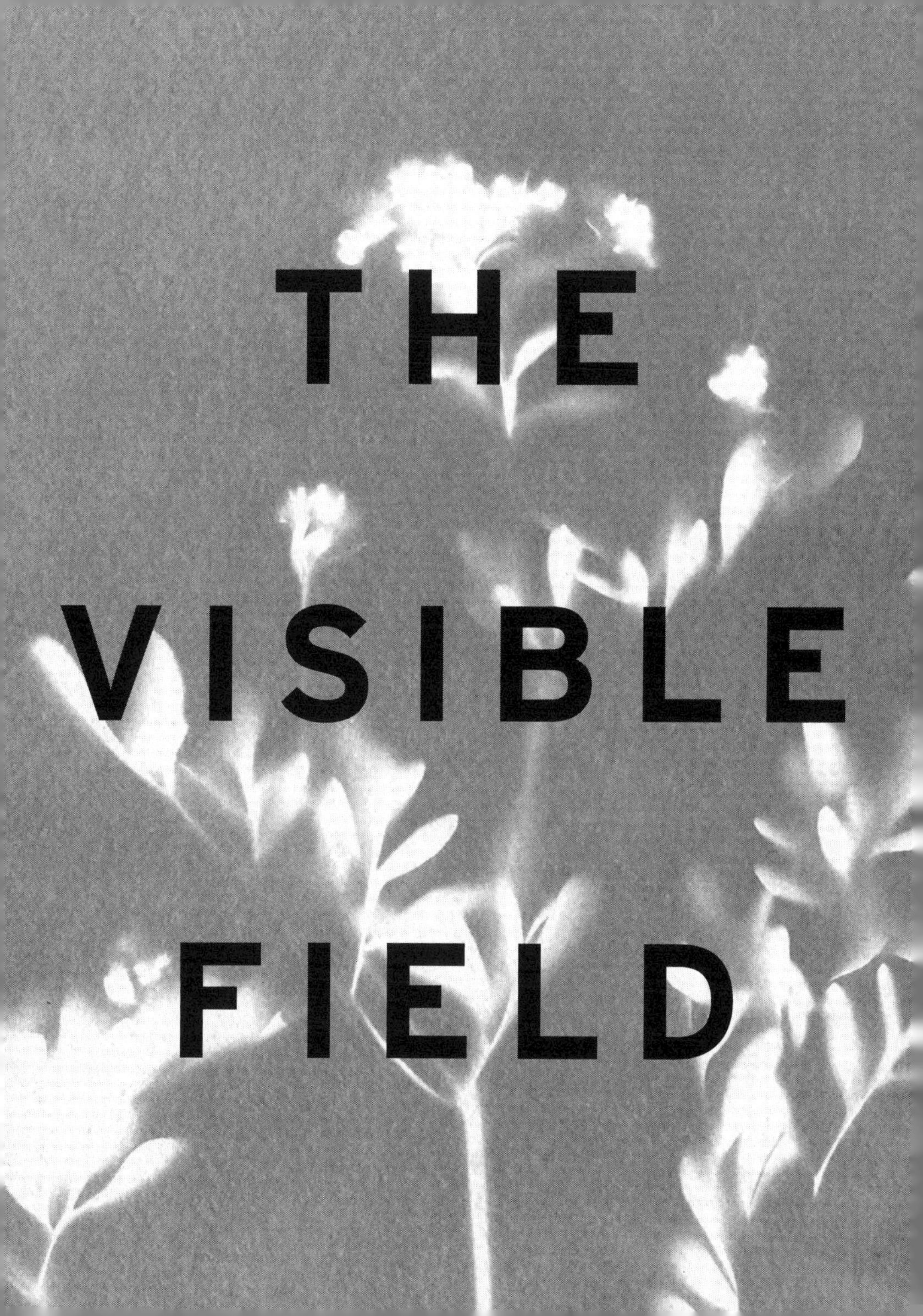

THE VISIBLE FIELD

Published in the United States of America

Library of Congress Cataloging-in-Publication Data
White, Zoë Ryder, 1974–
The Visible Field / Zoë Ryder White.
ISBN-13: 979-8-992611-6-49
Subjects: LCSH: American Poetry, Nature, Phenomenology
LCGFT: Poetry.
LCCN: 2025942188

Cover and interior design by Alban Fischer

RIVER RIVER BOOKS
10 Linganore Place
Durham, NC 27707

www.riverriverbooks.org

CONTENTS

Listen to yourself, the therapist said;
do you hear how you sound, she said,
and I heard the sound of a mare
trying to turn around
in a stall too small for turning.
Trying to know the other view.
This is not a metaphor
for an unhappy life.
This is how my body felt.
This is how neurology followed its groove,
showed me a picture of a mare
in a stall too small for turning.
Mare's shoulder pressed in one direction,
mare's flank pressed in the other.
The torque involved.
The stillness at the center.
And field in every direction:
visible field.

1.

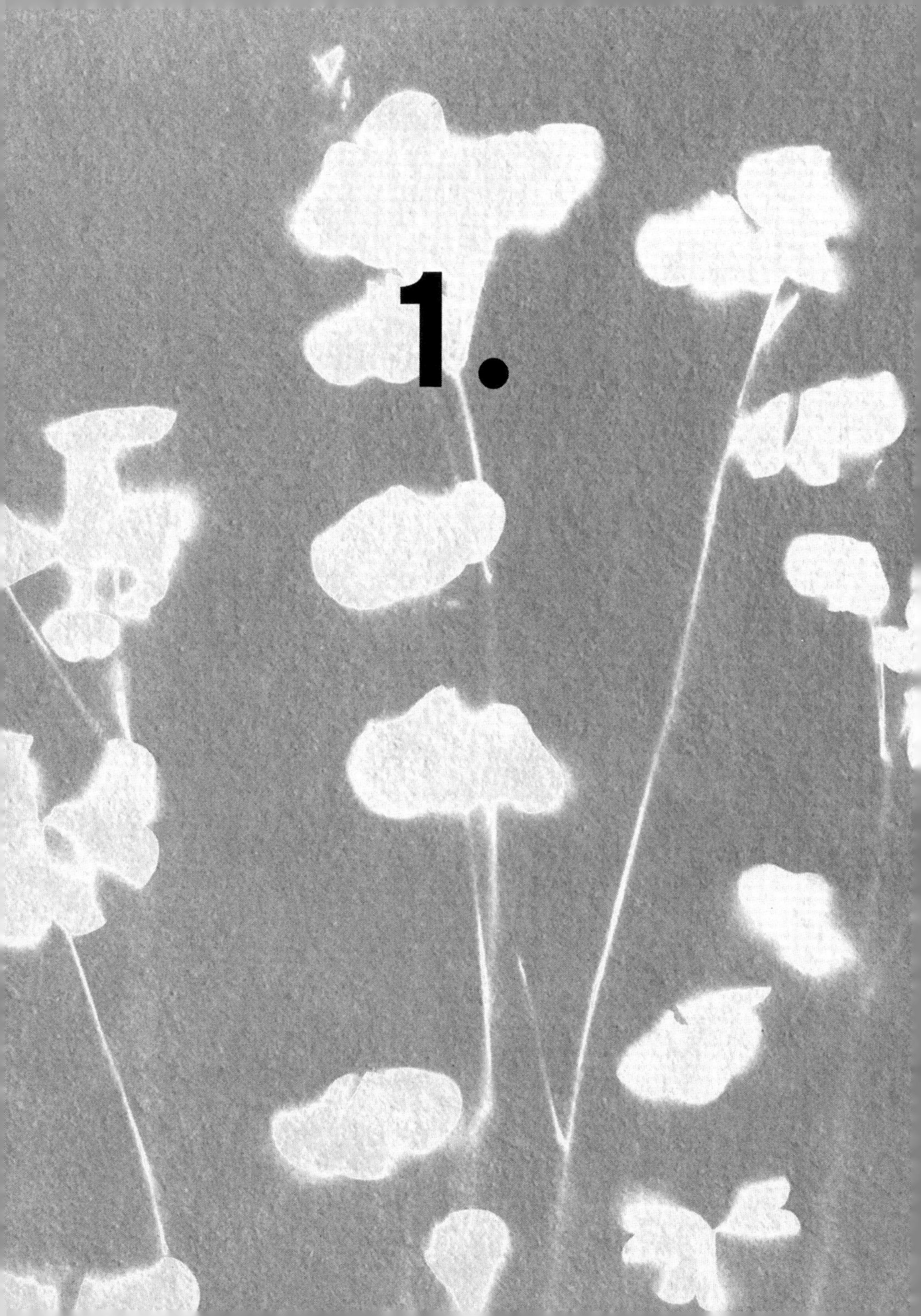

I was missing my antlers,

so you folded me a pair,
along with some other doubles—
doves; cuffs.

I have affixed
what you built
to my skull.

If what you want
to do with paper now
is crush it into balls,
lob two
in my direction.

The old plan was
to sit a spell,
then walk
in flammable quiet.

The new plan
is to trick the whale
into opening her mouth
and then we get in.

Ode to a Sears Electric Typewriter

Back then ink slapped
fast and hard, a smack,
a shot, each letter
indented, each *m* pressed fast
against paper's nap, each
wrong word visibly *x*'d,
a grove, a fence
between fields.
And the wind spun up
green and the grasses
were stirred and I was
just past girlhood, freckling,
astonished, the blurred world
caught in the thrash
of each branch, each word
cracked and shucked
by what was, and then gone,
as now is, as each year
cradles the last, and
the next, and
the next.

Girlhood

We used to walk along the freight tracks between Northfield and Dundas. The trains we stepped aside for carried taconite: marble-sized balls of iron ore from the Mesabi Range north and west of Lake Superior. Though we were but girls, we had pockets. We filled our pockets with balls of iron ore as we walked until our pants hung heavy on our hips; first the front pockets, then the back pockets, then the rolled cuffs. We were heavy, then, walking the sunshine between Northfield and Dundas. No one saw. Crows saw. We were held to earth. We were exhausted. The cereal factory saw when we walked through its burnt barley smoke. The taconite saw. It talked in our pockets. It was sun-warmed and then it was 98.6. In the winter we packed it in snow, we packed ourselves in snow, we loaded our pockets and stuffed our mouths. The monarchs saw, and left. The geese. The heaviness of girls walking somewhere, girls increasing in—the geese left, and the crows. We felt the itch of pin-feathers under our t-shirts, we ignored the itch. We plucked each other's eyebrows, pocketed what we'd pulled. Snow melted down our legs. We rubbed the feathers off because you aren't supposed to touch them but we touched them and the wings became translucent, inoperable. The empty barns saw. We stuffed hay into our clothes where we found gaps, receptacles. We talked to make more gaps. In went the heads of dandelions, and then we smelled like dandelions until we smelled like gasoline. We could never tell from one minute to the next what might—we could never tell one minute from the next, but as each passed we pressed harder against the earth because the earth didn't care; could take it.

Boone County

In dark we pitch a tent against what seems flattest.
Small rain at first. Puttyroot orchid. Hop clover.
Love in a puff, also known as balloon vine
also known as heart's only seed.

Dog circles, yowls into the blacker sections.
The dream is chevrons, blinkered set of red pegasi, taillights
draining south out of Cincinnati, otherwise
known as swords to plowshares, the smoke
from that smelting blown at a slant, young corn.

Various beebalms, berries, worts. Bluets and catchfly.
We wake to clammy light, tugged in a curve of swollen creek.
False garlic, otherwise known as crow poison.
The dream is a mat woven of cinnamon fern, you and I

bottles stuffed to the neck in silt, wet messages,
wild violets we've devoured, young milkweed
that wasn't dogbane, though our stomachs cramped.

Upper fork of Big Bone Lick meets with lower,
two-tined, drains downhill to the Ohio.
Arms akimbo, we survey what sunk.

Jelly ground once took mastodons, marrow and all.
What swallowed those, might we wake inside of? Waterbed.
Tuber, pelvic girdle, tusks for bedfellows, salt cured.
Clay banks make us heavy shoes.

That Bird

Redwing shouldering home,
shouldering far from home,
I know not but his red-capped
sleeves, his epaulets.
I know not but his beak, his black
bird tongue, spool of him
unwinding between each branch
and crotch until he ends.
I know not
but his end, of which
he may know nothing.
I am red inside; you, too.
I paint my boat that color,
I paint my cup.
What's tipping out
is what I want.
I could throw that bird if
I could catch that bird.

March Coming In

Before, I thought unrest was a house
to move through. And tomorrow,
and the after-days: a yellow window
blinking on and off from the smeared street,
a movement in the vacant lot
something living made. A movement
in the snow something living made,
a waking creature, a representative piece
of the whole, the soul
less embarrassing to talk about
than it once was, but still I'd rather
call it a bird who leaves
the weeds shaken, the snow
knocked down. Is it any righter
to name one's longing *dissembler,*
dismantler, spirit-level, almighty,
than it is to name it by the name
of what you'd most like
to touch? I still want
the worst weather most, the coldest
sea, rain driven against what I stand
behind, crows in the orchard.
And the wind, still winter: sometimes
it unmakes me and sometimes
it just shows me my own shape.

Letter Home from Halifax

For months, I have felt the edges of this land
to be an impervious, mossy lace. The brine
seeps in, the brine seeps out.
Outside town in ditches
and gullies, *balsaminaceae:* jewelweed,
every touch-me-not flinging itself
across some distance.
I could say I walk through the center
of the patch, arms outstretched.
I could tell you I love the smell
of drying rockweed with a side
of beer, the tiny hovering flies.
Coins in the dryer sing
a scraping, metal song,
here as they do anywhere.
What I am trying for is synthesis:
a gathering, a lingering of selves
to walk through each other's centers
like a hot wind.
Here in Halifax, the wind is bitter
and the blossoms bright.
The people in me keep me
up late talking, sometimes
laughing, carrying on until
light's first silver blade
cuts across the harbor.

Infrastructure

It's June again. Let's take our clothes off!
June, and all the streets in Brooklyn
have loud holes in their middles.
That's how I find them, that's how
I know they're streets. The hole
in front of me is gaping, gorgeous,
with its planks and palomino soil.
Let's get in!
The things we could do
in that rarified radon. The thuds
and hums the earth absorbs, kicks back.
These days, I don't sleep.
Black locusts down the block
are sizzling; your skin collects pollen;
you've gone completely golden.
The street-pole that holds the wires
is seeping pitch. I want to wrap it
in my arms! It's musical. Narcotic. Look,
I have tied a red-and-white bakery string
around my thumb, to remember this.

Other Machines

Down below the barge, the barge's wide bottom, the touch
and press of welded steel along the brackish channel.

Every vessel leaves here skinned in oil, dipped.
Below the pier, the pilings, the sunken barrel staves:

bones of birds who died in flight, sifted down. Full stop.
Sounds made in water make the water move a little—

not just where the sound comes out; everywhere.
And light hits the water top, but only some of it

goes farther. See the cranes, the rung metal? Engines
moving heavy objects with no effort, only sound?

Effort is for bees, for humans. But this humming's
all around. Rain dashed in your face: that fervor.

Mid-life

It was like the dream I'd had over and over
since childhood: walking from room to room
I see a door I don't remember.
And when I open it, I find the real house:
the house inside the house.
The one I've meant to live in all along.
It looks the same. It is not spectacular;
there is no money in it;
but I feel like I felt that time at the bar,
loosening my tie, spooning marrow
from cow bones split into oily boats.
Like the first hard sting when milk lets down.
A fork in an outlet.
What I mean to say is that after,
it was just like that dream.
I walked around the city.
Because it was the other city, the one inside,
the street was a sleeve I slid into.
In the bookstore, I couldn't see:
words gathered to the ceiling,
pelted my face like hail. I loved it,
and all those samaras landing in my wine.
Sometimes, since then, I feel this way
when I'm awake. It lasts
longer and longer:
the world, shucked, the world

inside the world, where the bees live.
They speak only of god, but the mud
means sex or something like it
when it hums.

To touch the deep clock

I fall asleep,
push in
through the front,
feel around.
It will be closer to my spine
than I imagine.
It will tremble in my hand
like a mouse
but I cannot hurt it:
all days uncoil
from this one's slow ratchet,
sun snuffed into a brick
I keep to remind me
but I never know
of what.

Firstborn

The long loop
was a field of anything in the wind.
The metronome, the metronym, my own hip.
Never thinking about thinking. No phoneme. Roe.
A little fire. Opposable thumb. The first dream
had honeybees and the five fingers folding,
unfolding. Phylum chordata! To each
their own caul, their curtain. This bone
is built to sink. I dreamed a ship,
didn't you? I missed you, I pined,
I left home to find
you out.

Room with Fan and Light Socket

Inside the day's pentameter, a silo
of stillness. A quiet distance
the other mammals sleep between, but
you can't drop a pin there.
You can't hear a pin drop.
Inside the day, a story of women
asleep on the couch.
Stoneware. Ellipse.
Women asleep in apartments,
in beds alone, curled inside
a lover's punctuation.
Inside the day, the dreaming, sun
on the late garden, light
on the floor of the sun-facing rooms, legs
entangled, horses across the street
breathing into each other's cupped ears.
We save up as we sleep.
Dimes pass through the small glass mouth
until the bottle is silver
through and through
and even the shooting range
won't wake us, even
the glass smash, pentameter
unspun, hand in a sleeping
hand in a sleeping hand.

Devotion

The girl you were walked the path
from church to parsonage to church to parsonage
the year there were so many gypsy moths
they fell across the dark dirt, made lace of it.
To get home without crushing one: impossible.
Your fervor is different from mine:
infused with thoughtful competence.
In the bath last week, you say, you set yourself the task
of watching snow melt into drops that hung
off the front yard dogwood.
Because you watched throughout
the fullness of each moment you had set aside
for watching, you got to see a lone bobcat exit the mist,
saunter behind the dogwood, down the middle of your road.
And then you were halfway to the living room,
calling your family to *look look look* out the window
before you noticed you had dripped a river down the stairs!
Jo, my reverent friend,
you know I never miss an opportunity to exclaim!
And while I am fairly certain this poem will embarrass you,
I write it anyway.

The Emily Dickinson Divination Deck

1.

Since I found this sleek box in the basement of Red Emma's and carried it home from Baltimore, I have been daily asking Emily to answer me. And she answers! Mornings, I pick a card; dark matter fills my hand: dark matter with a ring around, a deep green ribbon. Dark matter in a sachet, labeled at a fine tilt, baked in a bleak loaf, deep in the throat of the frog. I have come to keep a tin of it buried in the frozen field. Look, the room is filled with dark matter, the house entire, the rumpled yard, the children. It packs a ribcage, seeps. On each card's back, Emily's ruched Victorian bodice, her hands, her clasped nosegay (mignonette—gilly flower—alyssum). Look, dark matter in each pleat! In my buttonholes' gaps! Within each dark quadrant (so she tells me) of my heart. Emily gives the same news every day, though I ask any number of questions. She says, *you are who you are, who you ever, ever are.* I love her. I do. But she wears me out.

2.

What should I do, Emily, I ask.
Emily, how should I feel?
Last year's vine tendrils in my palm.
Last year's oat straw lit and burnished.
Red thorns,
dark droppings,
evidence of owls.
The precision of shale in ordered beds.
Small snow: rain-dimpled, frozen again.
Orchard bleak and keen.
Sometimes she's silent on any subject.

I label it "deafening rebuke."
The sky is blue in my throat again.
Windows bound in green.

3.
You could suck the air from any room
and press it in a ring box.
Though you leaned half out the window
in spirit, you tucked the rest in an apron pocket.
The tidy strips of paper you snipped
to paste the stems of flowers down! Why not
a nest, with those? Or was there one?
Sting and sweet, star-gulping lake,
the wine, the calyx, the daphne, the split
lobelia cardinalis surrounds. The card says
not to worry. God will write back,
in Their own hand, if I really *mean*,
when I mean.

Nitrogen

The book says a man discovered me
but I was not discovered, merely
pointed out.
Call me no-life, call me noxious,
call me burnt air, abundant
asphyxiant. I'll choke the life
out of your inefficient carotid
body, you won't know
that what you're breathing
is not air. Hey, I don't mean it! Here,
I'll make your war protection
and I'll make your war, your
superglue, amphetamine, refrigerant.
I'll both fertilize and fuck up
your field. I'm here to remind you
you're temporary, darling:
that sweet skin, those pink,
exquisite lungs. I'm here
to love you. I want
to suck you up. I know
the first approach can lead you
to experience significant repulsion
but keep trying; eventually
the charge goes nuclear enough
to overcome my awkwardness.
Really, I don't mean it!

Come here, let's make something
together, something violent,
something useful.

On Edna's Birthday,

I dreamed I stood on a classroom chair in the middle of spring telling X. I'd never loved anyone the way I'd loved X., never before or since. I proclaimed this falsehood in rhyming couplets: "searing" with "clearing," etc. The X. in the dream was an outdated version, hidden behind a tree. I don't know what X. looked like. I didn't care what X. said. It was my dream! It was all about me! *Tiresome heart*, Edna says. *House without air*, she says. "You're a Taurus with Sagittarius moon *and* rising," said X.'s voice from behind the tree, "no wonder." "Well, you're just an archetype," I sputtered, annoyed, searching for an impressive rhyme: overripe? Tuning pipe? Candystripe? Phenotype? I had an envelope of negatives in my back pocket; I left them at the base of the tree and woke up. Edna says *yellow*. She says *willow*. She says *popple*, she says *apple*, she says *hollow*. She once lived in a house barely wider than her shoulders. When she sang with her sisters, the neighborhood swooned.

Lasius Niger

My smallest daughter tells me she has learned a fact about ants that is so shocking, I should sit down. *The girls are in charge of everything*, she says. *They don't let the boys in their house!* After she is asleep, the computer tells me more facts about ants, so many things I didn't know—the queen's one day to fly, the mid-air mating and instant death of her partner, feeding herself on her own reabsorbed wings, the unfolding years of egg-laying and mastication underground. Great kindness between the ant wives, my daughter has told me. Cooperation. Minus the occasional fight to the death, she seems to be correct. Of the 88 officially recognized constellations, we have a sea goat, an air pump, a graving tool, a crow, two crowns, and Berenice's hair. Canis major and minor, but there is no ant. This seems foolhardy. Imagine spending the afternoon doing nothing but harvesting honeydew, carrying it home to your mother without thinking of anything but her appetite, extending.

To Make a Poem

1.

That we burn blue like a beer sign,
gas range in the night kitchen,
undoing a strap;
to step over the tub's lip, sink.
In the bath: bouquets of mussels,
the cutting lip, the crushed herb,
the city's first snow
caught in an envelope.
We displace our own shape,
soaking, reclaim it as we step out.
The water searches around,
but we're walking.
That we leave behind
a rime of salt and gilt.
That we are lit, like a yolk.

2.

We charcoal
a life-sized horse
on butcher paper;
cut around its edge
with safety scissors.
We want to make it
stand, move, eat.
When it folds

on its narrow ankles,
we poke it full of holes,
tie it to a string.
Run.
The paper body unfurls,
lifts above the field;
tugs, snaps on its line.
The horse's shadow
gallops over our bodies,
their shadows.
Hooves drum solid earth.

Entropy

is the only law of physics that isn't time-agnostic. Meaning, it can't be undone. This minute's chaos, each miniscule undoing, won't reverse. Meaning, S=K log W, "arrow of time," etc.: the minutes drive disorder but not disorder's opposite. Meaning, the Orionids sizzle through the heavens, one right after the next. I can't see them; it's cloudy, there's a hill I'd have to climb, plus I'm not wearing clothes, my hair is wet. The minutes nudge against each other in line. They made it dark. They changed my body. I'm jealous of their soft familiarity, their casual urge forward, the tender way they shove. The Orionids are lonely like the rest of us but the minutes are always in company. They bump along, undoing, undoing. The man who made the math was so struck with anguish (nothing stays, nothing stays) he left fast, via rope, via hotel doorframe. The hotel was in Duino, of all elegiac places, where the angels don't listen, or we think they don't. Stars imploding, stones pitching into the sea, a woman in the next room stepping out of her slip, one hand on the sill.

On the corner of Dikeman and Van Brunt, Jessica stops walking and tells me to knock it off, and she means my new habit of reflexive tabulation. *You've been speaking in spreadsheets since we crossed the Gowanus*, she says. *You think it's in service of meaning-making, but some questions don't have answers.* But I feel like a split plum, I say. I want to be a whole plum. *At least you feel like a plum*, she says. *You *could* feel like a box of sawdust. A fishbone. A fishbone stuck in a throat!* She has a point. If we walk a few more blocks we'll see saltwater. I could spit in it, it wouldn't matter. It's so big. I start to say, if I spit in the harbor, the water-movement necessary to propel my DNA below the Verrazano and out to sea is in inverse proportion to the motion needed to alternate between a sense of dissipation of self and a sense of acute concentration—see also: too much//not enough—but she suggests I might want to lighten up. *It's a beautiful day!* She says. *You're a bowl full of plums! Enjoy!*

What's melting isn't melting fast enough for me.

What would the ecstatics say?
Either don't get drunk, or do, but if you tongue the battery,
you will end up with a tender mouth—
not the worst outcome of faith in the unseen.
I forget whose tracks are whose, here, but the places we walked
have turned to ice, branches magnified in their ice envelopes,
room skewed. It's not any of you. It's my dumb machine,
my own chapped thumb.
When the power strip exploded last week,
the lamp didn't, the computer didn't.
So I guess it served its holy purpose.

For example,

I can't know
what you think about
as you fall asleep.
It's like the bird
in the tiger's throat:
I think I know
its position.
I think I see
its feather-color,
red in the dark
interior. But
I am wrong
about this color.
Such a human trick
to try to know.
To not. Over
and over.

The Mare

has no depth perception.
The mare has the largest eye
of any land mammal.
Standing still, the mare can see
clear around the world, except
for one hidden place
at the base of her tail.
The universe looks like a lake
when she dreams it.
When she dreams it,
the surface is still.
Sometimes the women
row to the dock,
peel off their shirts.
In they go: one, two, three.
The women do not know
they live in the mare's blind spot;
in her dream; below the whorl
between her eyes.

Most of the money had been stolen.

The city smelled fried, like stone, like oil on iron.
Do you know this story? There are humans in it.
One was comfortable giving pleasure, was given pleasure by giving pleasure.
Put your hands behind your back and let me, said the other, *put your hands above*,
and this was harder: the self scrolled down to a brass tack.
The self everywhere, unforgiving. The self's sweat in the self's eyes.
Windows the size of church doors opened above the street.
Let me, said the other, and it was harder, but not impossible.
On the paper map, they'd drawn a pencil line
down the center of streets that led to the sea.
The city smelled like almond blossoms and thyme.
Soot collected on anyone's shirt-sleeves, feet.
It was such a long walk.
Now, they had a few coins in a glass. Sunburn. The leftovers.
Clouds banked up against the ceiling, spun with the slow fan.
The self left a soot face-print on the white cloth before bed.
Everything would be different, after this.
Like eating a plum or a peach without a napkin.

Argument

Let us posit here that every truth
cradles a small lightless place within it,
such that I do with my dark space what I will;
you, etc. with yours.
It is such that I say out loud to myself
that the plum tree will make plums again
with their own dim rooms inside
though the yard between here and there is ice,
soot, dog shit. Let us further this discussion
with quantities of distilled spirits.
I am not convinced the plum tree
will make plums again, and this is why
I admonish myself out loud:
Take the long view! Anything can change!
Take the cleaner wrasse
with its blackened tongue.
Each one born female, but after that,
they shift as the mood strikes them.
Take the human animal.
There is a figurative hollow
just in from the hip.
Another at the base of the skull.
There's an overgrowth.
It isn't a secret.
I'll tell it to any of you.
I'm getting older

and less embarrassed; my blushing
doesn't make me blush.
It's not that I don't *care* what you think,
it's that it doesn't bother me.
When I was a fishwife, I married
the fish. The cleaner wrasse! She shifts
as the mood strikes her; the mood
strikes her, she shifts.

Before

When I was an envelope, I enclosed
a red scrap:
say what you want, you know
what its shape was.

When I was the scrap
I'd never slept
so soundly, had never
been quartered
so close.

2.

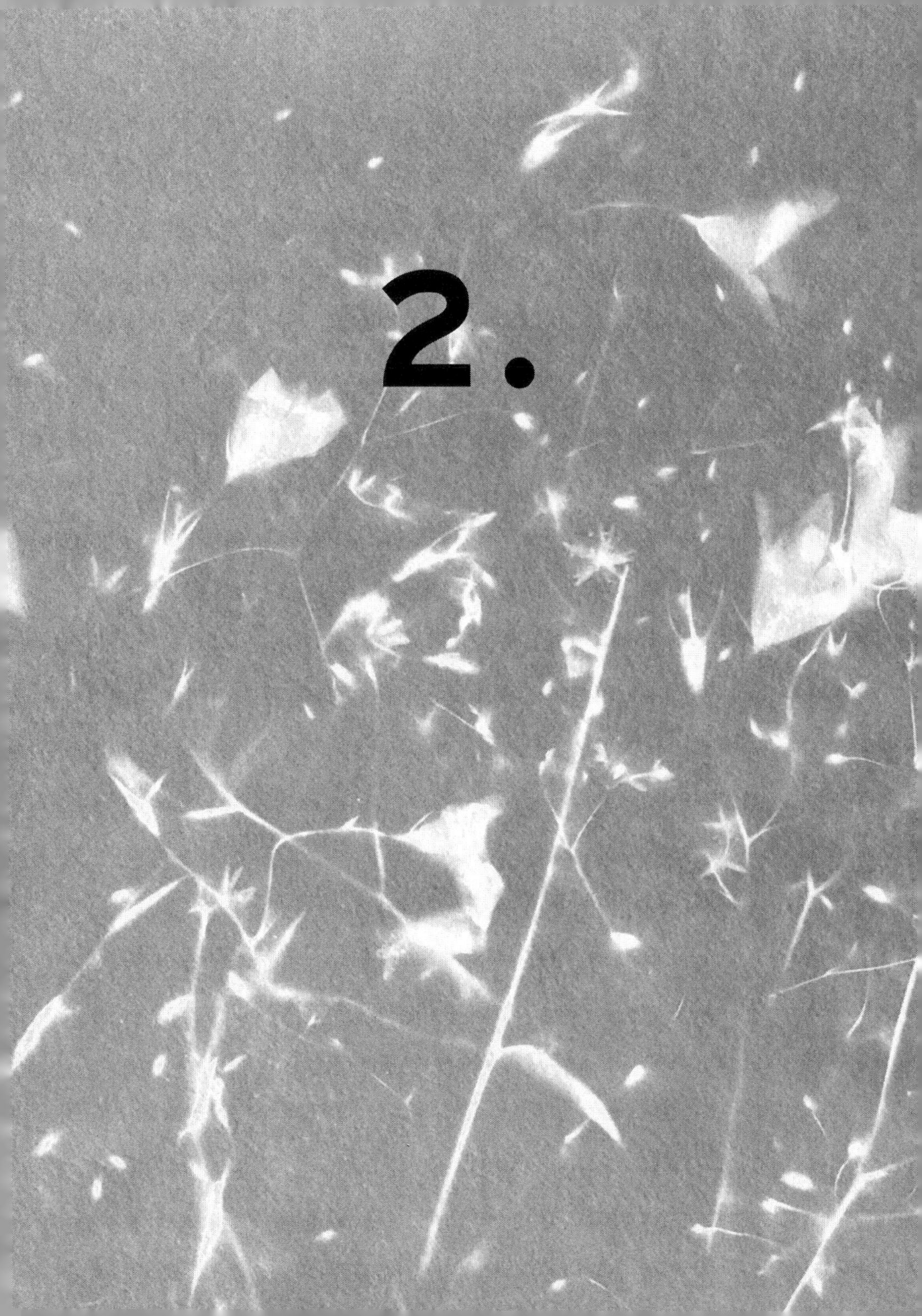

It seemed wrong

to take the book apart
but I took it apart. The cover
just cardboard at the core,
and all the yellowed glues
and string unstrung.
You were there. Each page
hung on the line.
The line hung.
The book reads differently now.
Beyond reason
is the only way to love,
it says. It says to go back
to the nursery,
buy the wan tree.
It says the moon
turns to face us,
illuminates the manuscript
of your shirt.
On the collar,
something four-legged.
Botany at the tail.
To read out of order
is to arrange one's affection
deliberately. Wind
hits the paper
and it swings.

Every animal

"Every animal is sad after coitus, except the human female and the rooster."
—GALEN, 2nd century Greek physician

I speak not for roosters' capacity
for tristesse. Spurred and gilded,
brutes with brains the size of thumbnails.
"A man's thumbnail," actually,
the article says. Who am I to speak
for anyone who hasn't asked?
Maybe the women Galen knew
took themselves to the seashore within,
were unmoved while he did what he did.
Watch the little boat with the little red sail
drop anchor. Watch the woman plummet.
Sad is a simple word, no? In the present tense,
she releases a swarm from her hand.

Oh to be happy in a body

with a body beside me.
I once owned a postcard that said
FEEL NO GUILT IN YOUR DESIRE.
Sometimes, walking to the grocery store,
I'd remember, and feel comforted.
It's like smelling the lake water
before you even get there.
To fit together
as water surrounds a swimmer.
No schematics. Biodiversity!
To become multiple. To multiply.
To swelter. To think about
the horse's velvet lip.
To think about the cropped weed.
To be taken between the other's teeth,
to take the other thus, to remain
unharmed, but different.
Quenched, but thirstier.

Full stop

Black dart to the heart
of my space between
spaces, pushpin you, sharp
on the side I can't see.
Sailcloth held firm
by your thorn, you gather
and you separate; you
frugal brigand,
you secretive spike.
You serve as warning,
piece shreds into a sky,
you fold the ends of everything
and fasten them.
You flint-in-the-eye.
You freckle.
You element, condensed.
I squirm
beneath your certainty,
your sure, deliberate touch.
How would I live
without you.
How do I, sometimes,
do, I sometimes
do

Halfty-half

The twins have invented a number, they tell me on the ride home. It is the number halfty-half. Do you mean one fourth, I ask, but they do not mean half OF half. Their elder sibling says it must be five point five. Or fifty five. But they say no, those are already numbers. Ray says halfty-half is bigger than eleven. Ivy says you can't count to it, though. What do you count with it, then, I ask. What do you measure? Ray says deer, but he might just be saying that he sees some, where they always are, just outside the prison fence. Yes, Ivy says. Also, water. In the rearview mirror I see them turn from their windows to look at each other. Inscrutable, mirthful, private.

Reading the Scan

The doctor looks tired as she walks me through layers of my son's skull, first from the outside in, next from the inside out. What does she see? I see where the crack begins and where it ends. His skull from this angle is thin and white as the lip of a cup. This surprises me. The doctor says the fracture extends through the glenoid fossa, traverses the anterior margin of the left carotid canal. Ossicles intact, my son lays sideways in the elevated chair listing the attack moves of Pokémon: *Absorb, Endure, Amnesia, Astonish.* The doctor says the left vestibular aqueduct is not enlarged. *Belch, Glacial Lance, Hurricane, Incinerate.* She says the fracture is as evident now as it was the day he fell. *Acid Armor, Fairy Wind, Venom Drench, Fissure.* She says she cannot see the nerve, but the auditory canal is patent, the Prussak space is clear, the scutum is sharp. *Confide, Heart Swap, Hold Hands, Scald.* The mastoid air cells are finally clear. *Dark Void, Mud Slap, Ominous Wind, Fake Tears.* Because his left eye will not blink on its own, my son uses his hand to blink it, many hundred times a day. He has become accustomed to this. He wants french fries. He wants to go home. What now, I ask the doctor. Just wait, the doctor says. Keep waiting. *Seismic Toss, Bonemarang, Synthesis, Hex.*

Quarantine 9

How beautiful the spent annuals,
tied to their roots. The yard's dense mud.
The viral load, the unscrolled breath.
Clouds have come down to touch us.
They hang around; they will not leave.
We have enclosed the yard with strings of light.
In this way, we are kept company.
In this way, our company is kept.

Lunar Retreat

Every year the moon slips farther away from here:
four centimeters for every three hundred sixty-five days.
The length of an entire newt! Every year.
Don't go!
Everyone speaks this from out of our sleep.
We're never simultaneously awake on earth,
so it's never not being said.
Do you hear those geese in the dark?
Down here the men are trying to build robots who think
like men think.
Remember the days we were happy
to pump our tanks full of diesel?
I am able make a limited number of animals from paper
(frog, wolf, crane)
but they can't even breathe on their own.
The moon is pulling.
That makes the air organize
in an aimed way, like rain.
The poet says she knows it's done
when it stops bothering her.
I've come to the bottom and still
I can't sit still.

Jean, in the car, when we pass the graveyard, the children take note. They say the dead people are always still there, and also still not-there. The graveyard is always there when we drive back and forth and back and forth to where we are going. It seems an absolute, but it isn't, is it, Jean. Once, last year, Ivy said, mom, good thing you have three kids, so that if one of us goes to the grave, you'll still have two left. You have gone to the grave, Jean. In the mornings in the fall and in the spring around here, the little river makes its own cloud. A low, serpentine one. Since the road follows the river, it follows the cloud. Sometimes we go in, sometimes we go out. When we go in, the twins open their windows and stick their hands out. I'm touching the cloud! I let the cloud in the car, they say. Do you hang around rivers? Did you have time to know you were going, when you went? There are a few different ways to get where we are going, when we drive back and forth, and I like to switch it up. Sometimes we watch a comb of rain drag across the field. Sometimes deer flashing their white warning: *I'm leaving*, they say. Did you say that, when you left? What did you say? I think to ask your daughter this question, but that is not the right question for a stranger to ask someone's daughter.

Driving south, my husband says: *Maybe we agree more about the way things are than it seems on the surface*, he says. I love how he keeps having the "best ever" of any number of experiences over and over again. *This is the best ever swim in the Atlantic*, he says, shivering, up to his knees in rockweed. *Never has the water been so much like water.* Every holiday, the best holiday, with the deepest holiday essence. And sex! Never have I enjoyed so much the sensation of sensation, he says. For a person who spends a lot of time attempting to dismantle the self, he does seem happy in a body. Even if what we see as real is as similar to reality as a computer desktop is to a desk. It's a dimensional thing, isn't it? The body beyond the body, undoing, the body falling through the body, expanding backwards from the body's representation of a navel. He sails around in there. I went up to the stand of ash by the orchard just now because I didn't want to miss anything. Never have I seen such yellow, I told him when I returned. The wind has never been air-in-transit as purely as it pushed against me up there. And the leaves! Never have they detached so completely from the branch, or broadcast themselves around the woods with such unplanned force.

Two Examples:

There is a stain under the dining room table where the cat released a chipmunk's blood sometime in August. This was not a typical scene. It was all of the blood the animal had; it pooled and sat overnight. It soaked into the floor. The next morning, cleaning it up, I felt distinctly alive, which is not to say exhilarated, just that I felt very different from what was left of the chipmunk. Though I am also very similar to the chipmunk, in ways too plentiful to note here, that is not what I was thinking at the time. The cat also left a certain organ untouched on the floor, as he always does. I don't know what the organ is but he leaves it neatly intact. It looks something like a tiny bagpipe, without the pipes. Speaking of stained things, I suppose you read about the recent defacing of the Scala dei Turchi? Bright red on the white cliffs! Visible from miles away! The whole town came out to hoover up the anomaly that same day, to restore the cliffs to their pristine state. Among the many examples of brutality a person could list in a poem, these (the chipmunk, the cliffs) are two. They are comparatively slight.

Conditional

If I feel more like sex when I am underfed it is not as good
as when I feel more like sex because I am gluttonous.
If then is implied.
If then's there, the sentence levers, see saws.
If I can't get my mind around the binary.
Bury the then. Prefer the pendulum. If I bury the then.
If the flakes fall up, they fall up: a rent down pillowcase.
If the pillowcase is rent, if the hens line their nests.
If the body is living the body is aging if the body
is aging the body is living if the body is irrelevant
who is happier. To use the body to forget it.
If I forget it and then remember again.
If I am startled by what I find. If I lose my appetite.
If my appetite governs my afternoon.
If I make use of it. If I am used.
If I am trying to reach somewhere, if I am trying not to,
if something is conjured up. If a body forms,
is it yours? Is it mine? If we're talking about love.
If the axiom's undone. Where are you?
If your herd/your flock/your swarm. If your kindling.
If your drove. If where in the midst of animals.

Will no one pick up the killed cat on 208?

She has been there for days.
She is in front of no one's home
but we all see her there
as we drive to and from our own.
Will no one move her?
The moon is waxing gibbous,
her coat is getting dirty, her paws
covered with salt.

It is either late or very early

when Jean and Jim come in through the bardo
to visit Nicole and me; separately, at the same time.
Jean behind me in the city bus.
Jim with that soft scarf
leading him into the restaurant.
I thought you were dead, I say to Jean.
That was before, she says.
Nicole opens her pocket-sized window.
She rests it on the classroom table
so I can hear what Jean is saying about poems
while I look around the city for my son.
He hasn't gone far, Nicole says, and I hear her
though I am several blocks away.
Then: everyone involved wakes up.
Later, at the table, my son says,
I was looking for you in my dream.
I was looking for you in mine, I say.
We sit there smiling.
His plate and hands dashed with sunlight.

Like Louise

I want to wear the rumpled button-down like Louise,
to wrap you in my many arms, mid-air,
to be that heavy and that suspended.
Resistance and yield,
yield and resistance.
To wear away what isn't you
to find you, talk to you, tend to you.
I want to dress in black and white like Louise,
to commit to formal ambiguity
as a map to follow
when stepping off the road.
The green patch is the place for couplings,
Untitled.
To have reached up to the shoulder joint
is to have become the meat inside the shell.
To wear the iron crown.
To wrinkle.
To muscle closer to "it,"
to "you."

Some sentences, some clauses, a word.

It took a long time to cross the room.
The room was so long.
The room had no ceiling because the house had no roof.
The floor was uneven.
Any round thing set on one side would roll to the other.
There was a collection of roundish objects to the left.
The windows were difficult to discern because there were no walls.
Some of us could hear the dead only as we started walking or just before we got there.
Others heard them all the time: singing, carrying on.
Below the floorboards, below the space below the floorboards: relics.
A cache of seeds and plastic.
Snow in a spilled globe.
The cast-off, spooned bones.
No longer necessary.
Necessary for such a short time.

Interview

After Bhanu Kapil, "Twelve Questions"

The fish, when split, had a belly full of plastic, but it was still a fish.
I sifted up from the bottom with the motor in my ear.
The heron forgot it had legs at all, once it left the lake.
I am always wanting to take things off and leave them in piles to walk away from.
I will do that, to begin.
I will take the pin from the hinge's middle.
I will bury that in the hole that is for shouting into.
I will live by walking. Also by standing still.
That is too many I's in a row.
The shape of the body can be felt even if it cannot be seen.
The shape is made by the tracks the walking makes,
as seen from above; as seen from below.
Who is responsible? I leave my mother out of poems.
I am responsible.
I have been trying to get the sawblade through the green board,
but the green board's sap and swelling make the saw stick.
I remember sifting up from the bottom with balls of taconite in my pockets,
and the train coming and the train leaving and the wind stirred up from that.
If I say nothing, no one will know where I am.
When I say I want to take things off of me
I mean the knotted net—not the lip, not the limb.
I know I am not a fish.
One morning, it was still dark when I woke on the pine needles.
The barred owls weren't far away. My family was breathing.

I listened for each of them breathing; I heard each of them breathing.
I practice being bodiless.
I use my body for this exercise.

Unsent

Dear disturbance, I wonder how you are in your acute middle age far away on the other side of the

Dear existential dread, my computer is missing an H, I have to hover my finger over the spot where it sat; it's not much like typing—I give the machine a little bit of my electricity and the machine gives me an H, and so we

Dear rupture, I dreamed I spilled a bottle of green ink on the polished white floor of the five and dime and left without telling, without

Dear lookout, remember when we lived in the fire tower and never saw any fire we hadn't set ourselves, but we kept ourselves busy that way, setting and dousing and setting and

Dear synapse, we were so impulsive, we're lucky to be alive and well if estranged in the same way I am estranged from the perfect spelling of my youth; I can't remember irregularities or irregularities are the only

Dear vault, you leak in the mornings; nothing tangible, nothing to write home about, just, a little mist at the seams, a chord, the gentle sounds a clock makes, a

Dear swimmer, the Atlantic becomes you, inscrutable green frock; what you've been wearing weighs nothing, makes no sound when you move; while we were occupied with other matters, a forest grew between

Counting Blackbirds

From inside the murmuration I texted Jo. I am inside these birds, I wrote. I sent a seven-second video. *OH!!* Jo wrote back. The birds lifted in sequence from their several trees, lit again on several others a little farther down the hill. I felt the air they beat on my face and hands. I felt my heart's indecorous thud. How many landing blackbirds, and no one missed their branch! Then they were gone. Since they were gone, I started running. I thought to text Jo later: is there a finite number that represents how many times a person might stand inside a flock? *What if this is my fourth-to-last time???* But maybe the issue is less a scarcity of murmurations than a scarcity of imagination, of action plans. Running down the ridge, I thought, I need not passively accept my own projected lack of blackbird. I could just go to where the birds are, and be still. But where had they gone? At bedtime tonight, my son said *a number is a number is a number and it goes on forever. Ever is a number*, he said, *and every number also has its word.* He asked, *what is the difference between the number alone and the word we say for it?* It irks, that distance. The birds are darts, are darning needles, are gasps of sorrow, are bickering in the bare trees, are gripping bark, are gorging on seeds, are sparks on the wire, are gone again, lifting as you stumble through their cloud.

Errata

Where the book says hair, read smoke pulled into the low places.
Where it says low places, read until urged elsewhere I will stay.
Where it says gathering, read, I am watching them reach.
I am taking their temperature. I am trying that temperature on.
For foil, read I am become the electric range.
For winter, read I open my shirt to the empty room.
For several weeks, read: the room fills with hot air, tugs up
like the swim bladder maneuvering the fish.

Solstice

I want to say I recognize everything, but I don't, not even the house
moving across the yard like a lit ship as I walk back from shutting in the hens.
Not even the hens do I recognize. The noises they make roosting
mean love or comfort or nothing, or, *it is time to make these noises*
because we can no longer see. I shut the hens in, and the house shifts slowly
over the yard like cruise ships used to ease across rectangles of daylight
at the ends of avenues in Red Hook. I aim my walking home
for where the house is and for where the house was and for where the house
could be. There is no *ending up* anywhere, even for the cat I buried yesterday.
That digging made me sweat. The cat's weight: a ream of paper
in a closed cardboard box. The dark in the box joined the dark in the hole
joined the dark the night made. My friend texts this word: *ecliptic*,
a noun, the great circle the earth's orbit makes where it intersects
the celestial sphere. The face of my phone illuminates,
another lit plane. It's getting cold on this slice of sky. In the coop,
one bird's head tucked beneath the next bird's wing. Close quarters.

ACKNOWLEDGMENTS

Grateful acknowledgement is made to the editors of the following journals, wherein versions of these poems first appeared:

Bellevue Literary Review: "Reading the Scan," "On the Corner of Dikeman and Van Brunt"

Iterant: "Entropy," "It seemed wrong"

Plume Anthology 10: "Like Louise"

Salamander: "That Bird," "March Coming In"

Sixth Finch: "Listen to You," "Halfty-half," "Girlhood"

SOFTBLOW: "Letter Home from Halifax"

SWWIM: "Counting Blackbirds"

The Leavings: "Conditional"

Willow Springs: "Interview," "Lunar Retreat," "Some Sentences, Some Clauses, a Word"

Thank you to Han VanderHart and Amorak Huey of River River Books for shepherding this collection so thoughtfully into being. This press was worth waiting for, and I'm forever grateful for your vision and care, and for your profound commitment to (and obvious delight in) poets and poetry. Thank you to Alban Fischer for this breathtaking design.

I'm grateful to the extraordinary poets who took time from their lives to think and write about these poems. Lauren Camp, Vijay Seshadri, and Bianca Stone, thank you.

I'm grateful for the decades of companionship I've found in various collectives, poetry clubs, poem-a-day documents and text threads. Even when poetry is lonely, one need not be always alone.

Thank you to Nicole Callihan, my forever collaborator—we've been writing alongside each other for nearly thirty years now. This book owes a debt of gratitude to our collective adventures of thought, your diligent nudging, these decades of friendship. Let the romp continue. Thank you to Caitlin McDonnell for your floating dock and your forthrightness, your ferocity and fun, in poems and in life. Thank you to Joanna Solfrian and Jennie Panchy for our writing days, our mid-way meet-ups, for sublime conversations I never want to end. Thank you to Iris Jamahl Dunkle for the loving motivational speeches and for always cheering me on.

Terence Degnan and Denver Butson, my brothers in poetry, each did a careful read of an earlier version of this manuscript and offered astute feedback. Thank you.

To all of my parents, especially my mom, Tripp Ryder, thank you for infusing my life with books, and for modeling a rich and active life of the mind.

Paul, my love and partner in life, thank you for space to write poems and for kitchen table conversations about consciousness and physics and soup stock and who is picking up which child where. You make me laugh and you make me think. I am the luckiest duck.

Florian, Ivy and Ray: being your mom is life's best thing.

NOTES

"Firstborn" is for Florian White

"Room with Fan and Light Socket" was indirectly inspired by staring at Elizabeth Bishop's painting, "Cabin with Porthole"

"On Edna's Birthday," refers, of course, to Edna St. Vincent Millay

"*Lasius Niger*" is for Ivy Grace White

"Halfty-half" owes a debt of gratitude to Odysseus Sheppard-Gould, who "the twins" have since told me is truly the originator of the concept of "halfty-half." Let this set the record straight!

"Reading the Scan" is for Ray Tobias White

The poet mentioned in "Lunar Retreat" is Mary Ruefle

"Jean, in the car" is for Jean Valentine

"Driving South, my husband says:" is for Paul Steely White

"Like Louise" refers to Louise Bourgeois

© ADRIANNE MATHIOWETZ

ZOË RYDER WHITE (she/her) has had poems appearing in *Tupelo Quarterly*, *Iterant*, *Plume*, and *Threepenny Review*, among others. Her most recent chapbook, *Via Post*, was a finalist for Tupelo Press's Snowbound Chapbook award and won the Sixth Finch chapbook contest in 2022. Her chapbook, *HYPERSPACE*, was the editors' choice pick for the Verse Tomaž Šalamun Prize in 2020 and is available from Factory Hollow Press. She co-authored *A Study in Spring* with Nicole Callihan. Another collaboration with Nicole, *Elsewhere*, won the Sixth Finch chapbook competition in 2019. A former elementary school teacher, she edits books for educators about the craft of teaching.

RIVER RIVER BOOKS was founded by Amorak Huey and Han VanderHart in March 2022. Inspired by the idea that you cannot step in the same river twice, two poetry editors join together to publish (at least) two exceptional poetry titles a year, as well as the Plainwater Nonfiction Series.

Poetry Catalog

An Eye in Each Square, Lauren Camp, 2023
Bullet Points: A Lyric, Jennifer A Sutherland, 2023
Dear Memphis, Rachel Edelman, 2024
A Geography That Does Not Hurt Us, Carla Sofia Ferreira, 2024
Pastoral, 1994, Joe Wilkins 2025
Your Mother's Bear Gun, Corrie Williamson, 2025
Field Notes, E.G. Cunningham, 2025
Encounters for the Living and the Dead, Jameela F. Dallis, 2025
Antibody, Elane Kim, 2026
House of Myth and Necessity, Jennifer A Sutherland, 2026
Scythe, Elizabeth Sylvia, 2026
Fifty Mothers, Preeti Vangani, 2026
The Visible Field, Zoë Ryder White, 2026
Snails of the Apocalypse, Martha Zweig, 2026
Turn a Girl to Salt, Janet McAdams, 2027
Little Automata of the Deciduous Forest, Mirande Bissell, 2027
Whale Garden, Carolyn Oliver, 2027

Plainwater Nonfiction Series

There Is News Along the Ohio River, Beth Gilstrap, 2026
Backyard Alchemy, J.D. Ho, 2026